ICKY BUG
COLORS

by Jerry Pallotta

Illustrated by
David Biedrzycki

SCHOLASTIC INC.

New York   Toronto   London   Auckland   Sydney   Mexico City   New Delhi   Hong Kong   Buenos Aires

Thank you to Vernon Hall.
— *Jerry Pallotta*

To Cathy Curbow, Greg Bozadjian, and Steve Arey for watching my little ladybug Julia.
— *David Biedrzycki*

Text copyright © 2002 by Jerry Pallotta.
Illustrations copyright © 2002 by David Biedrzycki.
ICKY BUG is a registered trademark of Jerry Pallotta.
All rights reserved. Published by Scholastic Inc.
SCHOLASTIC, and associated logos
are trademarks and/or registered trademarks of Scholastic Inc.

ISBN 0-439-38917-8

Library of Congress Cataloging-in-Publication Data available

12 11 10 9 8 7 6 5   3   4   5   6   7/0

Printed in the U.S.A   08
First Scholastic printing, September 2002

true bug

ant

spider

bee

dragonfly

grasshopper

moth

cicada

beetle

butterfly

fly

centipede

There are lots of different kinds of bugs.
Oops, the grasshopper jumped off the page.

Let's use bugs to learn colors. To see color, you need light.

It is really dark on this page. Please turn on the lights!

Thank you! That's better. Wow! Look at all the colors! These bugs are real. Bugs are the most colorful creatures on earth.

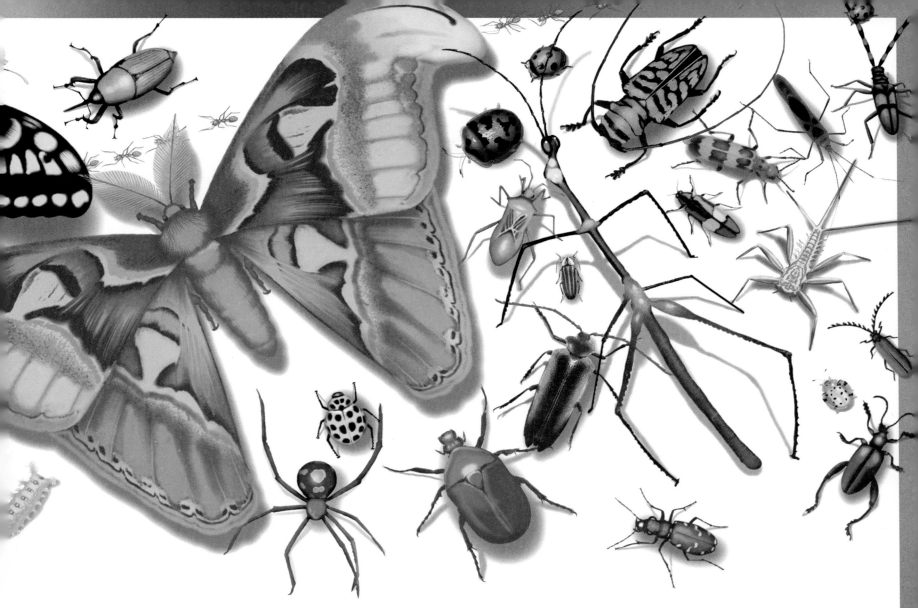

Coral reef fish are colorful. Flowers, birds, and frogs are colorful. But the colors and patterns of bugs are amazing!

People everywhere love to watch butterflies. They are graceful fliers that do not sting or bite. Butterflies have no teeth.

Butterflies are very fragile. If you see one, enjoy it, but do not touch.
Red butterflies are very rare.

yellow

Here are some true bugs. Some bugs drink nectar. Some bugs chew leaves. Some bugs have huge jaws. But true bugs have sucking mouths.

Another way to identify a true bug is by its wings.
True bugs fold their wings crisscross along their backs.

If you like the color blue, this weevil is for you!
Weevils are beetles that use their long mouths to eat
nuts, seeds, and berries. Beetles fold their wings in a
straight line down their backs.

Red, yellow, and blue are primary colors.
If you mix two primary colors together, you will get a new color.
Before we mix anything, let's explore the colors black and white.

Ants live together in huge numbers.
They work as a team for the good of the whole colony.

black

Insects have three main body parts.
It is easy to see the head, the thorax,
and the abdomen on these black ants.

What are they doing with the letters?
Bring those letters, b-l-a-c-k, back!

white

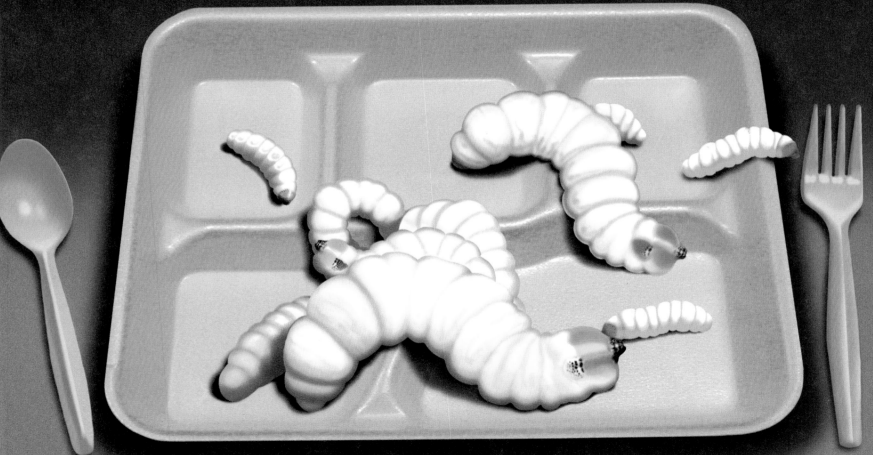

These white grubs are caterpillars.
They will grow up to be pretty moths, unless they get eaten first.

In many countries, people eat grubs. They can be eaten raw or roasted like a marshmallow. Someone ate all the grubs off this plate. Yum!

orange

If you mix the colors red and yellow, you will get orange.
This tiger moth has orange on its wings. Moths usually fly at night.
Butterflies almost always fly during the day.

The life cycle of a moth goes like this: egg, caterpillar, cocoon, moth.
Then the moth lays an egg and the cycle begins over again.

If you mix the colors blue and
yellow, you will get green.
Here are some green chrysalises.
Very soon a beautiful butterfly
will climb out and fly away.

green

The life cycle of a butterfly goes like this: egg, caterpillar, chrysalis, butterfly. Then the butterfly lays an egg and the cycle begins over again.

purple

Blue and red make purple.
These purple tortoise beetles
look grape-flavored.
A tortoise is a land turtle.
These beetles have a protective shell
that makes them look like turtles.

Beetles come in every shape, size, and color you can imagine. Beetles live in every neighborhood. They can be found in lakes, on mountains, in forests, in deserts, and even in your house.

Is clear a color? No!
Have you ever seen a clear crayon?
Probably not. Here is a dragonfly.
Its four wings are clear.
You can see right through them.

clear

Damselflies have clear wings, too.
Their wings are shaped like the letter X.
Damselflies can fold their wings back when they stop to rest.

If you add white to blue, you get light blue. If you add white to green, you get light green. If you add white to red, you do not get light red, you get pink.

pink

This pink orchid mantis is very sneaky. It looks like a pretty flower, but it attacks and eats any bug that comes nearby. This bug is camouflaged.

Count the legs
on this brown tarantula.

brown

One, two, three, four, five, six, seven, eight, nine, ten.
No! There are only eight. Spiders have eight legs.
The two things next to its mouth are called palps.
The palps help the spider catch and hold its food.

gold

Here is a gold metallic beetle. It looks like it could be worn as jewelry.
But, it is not really made of metal.

silver

And let's not forget the silver metallic beetles.
Gold! Silver! All we need now is a bronze,
and we can have the icky bug Olympics.